Would You Rather?
BIBLE
Questions

Would You Rather? BIBLE Questions

A Fun Bible Game for Kids and the Whole Family!

Clareese Saunders

Z KIDS · NEW YORK

Copyright © 2025 by Penguin Random House LLC

Penguin Random House values and supports copyright. Copyright fuels creativity, encourages diverse voices, promotes free speech, and creates a vibrant culture. Thank you for buying an authorized edition of this book and for complying with copyright laws by not reproducing, scanning, or distributing any part of it in any form without permission. You are supporting writers and allowing Penguin Random House to continue to publish books for every reader. Please note that no part of this book may be used or reproduced in any manner for the purpose of training artificial intelligence technologies or systems.

All rights reserved.
Published in the United States by Z Kids, an imprint of Zeitgeist™
A division of Penguin Random House LLC
1745 Broadway, New York, NY 10019, U.S.A.
penguinrandomhouse.com
zeitgeistpublishing.com

Zeitgeist™ is a trademark of Penguin Random House LLC.
ISBN: 9780593886120
Ebook ISBN: 9780593886052

Interior art © Shutterstock/JosepPerianes,
    Shutterstock/Perfect_kebab, and Shutterstock/Here
Cover art © Shutterstock/ivector
Cover design by Aimee Fleck
Interior design by Katy Brown
Author photograph © by Natalia Estrella
Edited by Caroline Lee

Printed in the United States of America

The authorized representative in the EU for product safety and compliance is Penguin Random House Ireland, Morrison Chambers, 32 Nassau Street, Dublin D01 YH68, Ireland. https://eu-contact.penguin.ie

1st Printing

To my great and late grandmother, Juanita Alinda Day.

You gave me curiosity. You gave me encouragement. Most importantly, you gave me Jesus.

This one is for you.

Contents

INTRODUCTION 8
HOW TO PLAY 10

ROUND 1 Nature 13
ROUND 2 Prophets and Disciples 23
ROUND 3 Dreams and Symbols 33
ROUND 4 Heroes! 43
ROUND 5 Battles 53
ROUND 6 Miracles 63
ROUND 7 Jesus' Birth, Life, and Death 73
ROUND 8 Parables 83
ROUND 9 Fruit of the Spirit 93
ROUND 10 Traditions 103

TALLY UP: SCORE SHEETS 114
WINNER'S CERTIFICATE 118
CREATE YOUR OWN! 120

Introduction

Welcome to *Would You Rather? Bible Questions*! Whether you are someone who has read the Bible front to back and upside down or has recently attended their first Sunday school class—this book is for you! This book has been designed as a game to encourage exploring your faith while having fun.

Although this book is structured to be played one way, do not be afraid to get creative! All you need is your curiosity. Since this book is meant for you, 8- to 12-year-olds and your families, remember this game is a great way to pick each other's brains, ask questions, and, of course, win, because is there anything better than outsmarting your parents and siblings?

Though our faith is never a laughing matter, I have found that my faith has grown best where we learn and have fun together. Hearing other players' answers helps us see we each have different ways of thinking, including the way *you* think!

This game challenges everyone. If you don't understand a reference or aren't familiar with every story—fear not! That just means you are playing the right game. Each question also has Scripture references so you and your family can dig deeper to uncover all the treasures within the Bible.

Speaking of the Bible, grab yours and your nearest and fiercest competitors, because the time has come for some faith and fun!

Are you ready?

On your mark, get silly—Go!

How to Play

Now that you have gathered your competition, I mean, your loved ones, it is time for a game of humor and honesty. Everyone is welcome!

This game is played in 10 unique rounds of 17 questions each.

Taking turns as judge, read the questions aloud to the group. Discuss and pick the funniest, wisest, or most creative answers and explanations. If you want to keep score between players, establish a winner for each round and use the pages starting on page 114 to keep score. When all rounds have been completed, tally up and determine the champion.

In the event of a tie, answer the tiebreaker question on page 113. All remaining players will vote on the best answer. If only two people are playing, whoever has the funniest or most thoughtful answer wins. The winner of the most rounds is the champion!

At the end of the book, you'll also find empty entries. Get creative and record your own silly "Would you rather?" questions and freely incorporate them into your game!

Here are some other ways to play:

- **Trivia style:** Challenge one another to guess what book of the Bible the question comes from. Level up and guess the chapter and verse!

- **Charades style:** Act out each question to outsmart the opposing team

- **Conversation style:** Simply use the questions as conversation starters or icebreakers to get to know one another, no need to keep score.

Nature

Would you rather

be a lamb that is roommates with a wolf

OR

a cow that sleeps in the same field as a lion?

ISAIAH 11

Would you rather

be a seed inside the first fruits in the Garden of Eden

OR

a tiny mustard seed that will grow into a large tree?

GENESIS 1 & MARK 4

Would you rather

count and name all the stars in the night sky

OR

all the wild animals and birds on the earth?

PSALM 147 & GENESIS 2

Would you rather

be small and have the wisdom of an ant

OR

be large and have the roar of a lion?

PROVERBS 6 & PSALM 104

Would you rather

see the rivers clapping their hands

OR

hear trees singing for joy?

PSALM 98 & 1 CHRONICLES 16

Would you rather

have the Tree of Life

OR

the Tree of the Knowledge of Good and Evil in your backyard?

GENESIS 2

Would you rather

be the large fish that swallowed Jonah

OR

the fish that was multiplied to feed the 5,000?

JONAH 1 & JOHN 6

Would you rather

experience the strong wind of the Holy Spirit

OR

see Jesus speak and calm the wind?

ACTS 2 & MARK 4

NATURE

Would you rather

have God embellish you like he does the lilies of the valley

OR

lead you to rest in green pastures like the sheep?

MATTHEW 6 & PSALM 23

Would you rather

soar on the wings of eagles

OR

walk through the parted Red Sea?

ISAIAH 40 & EXODUS 14

Would you rather

live in the wilderness alone for 40 days and nights like Jesus

OR

wander through the wilderness for 40 years like the Israelites?

MATTHEW 4 & JOSHUA 5

Would you rather

try counting the cattle on a thousand hills

OR

all of the stars in the sky?

PSALM 50 & GENESIS 15

Would you rather

be a lizard living alone in the king's palace

OR

a bird living with all the other animals on Noah's ark?

PROVERBS 30 & GENESIS 7

Would you rather

be the donkey that carried Mary to Bethlehem

OR

the donkey that carried Jesus into Jerusalem?

LUKE 2 & MARK 11

Would you rather

be a river for people to drink from in the desert

OR

a rock that gushes water?

ISAIAH 43 & EXODUS 17

Would you rather

tell the ocean where to stop

OR

tell the sun when to rise?

JOB 38

Would you rather

be a tree with leaves that are always green

OR

a tree that always grows twelve different fruits?

JEREMIAH 17 & REVELATION 22

 **ROUND 1 WINNER**

_____

Prophets and Disciples

Would you rather

walk on water like Peter

OR

ride down the Nile in a basket like Moses?

MATTHEW 14 & EXODUS 2

Would you rather

win a battle with pots and trumpets like Gideon

OR

win it by marching and shouting like Joshua?

JUDGES 7 & JOSHUA 6

Would you rather

talk to God as a burning bush like Moses

OR

talk to the risen Jesus at the tomb like Mary Magdalene?

EXODUS 3 & JOHN 20

Would you rather

be thrown overboard into the sea like Jonah

OR

shipwrecked on a remote island like Paul?

JONAH 1 & ACTS 27

Would you rather
lead the Israelites into the Promised Land after Moses like Joshua

OR

lead the church after Jesus' resurrection like Peter?

JOSHUA 1 & ACTS 1

Would you rather
share about Jesus coming in the future like Isaiah

OR

tell the good news about Jesus paying for our sins like his early followers?

ISAIAH 9 & LUKE 9

Would you rather

be the one to bless King David with oil like Samuel

OR

praise Jesus with expensive perfume like Mary Magdalene?

1 SAMUEL 16 & JOHN 12

Would you rather

appear after death as a ghost like Samuel

OR

appear on the mountaintop like Moses and Elijah?

1 SAMUEL 28 & MATTHEW 17

Would you rather

see Elijah divide the Jordan River with his cloak

OR

see him command fire down from heaven?

2 KINGS 2 & 2 KINGS 1

Would you rather

help save a widow and her son with overflowing oil like Elisha

OR

help feed the 5,000 with multiplying fish and bread like the disciples?

2 KINGS 4 & MARK 6

Would you rather

share God's love to people in the wilderness like John the Baptist

OR

share God's love by visiting different cities like Paul?

MATTHEW 3 & ACTS 20

Would you rather

witness someone being raised from the dead like Thomas

OR

would you want to help raise someone from the dead like Elijah?

JOHN 11 & 1 KINGS 17

Would you rather

lie on your side for 390 days

OR

shave your head with a sword?

EZEKIEL 4 & EZEKIEL 5

Would you rather

have a meal with angels like Abraham

OR

have the Last Supper with Jesus like the disciples?

GENESIS 18 & MARK 14

Would you rather

have bones like Elisha that can bring someone back to life when touched

OR

see dry bones come to life like Ezekiel?

2 KINGS 13 & EZEKIEL 37

Would you rather

witness an angel shutting the mouths of lions like Daniel

OR

have an angel wake you up with a meal of bread and water like Elijah?

DANIEL 6 & 1 KINGS 19

Would you rather

have the wisdom of Deborah to settle arguments

OR

the knowledge of Priscilla to teach others about Jesus?

JUDGES 4 & ACTS 18

 ROUND 2 WINNER

_____

Dreams and Symbols

Would you rather

have your breakfast delivered to you by ravens like Elijah

OR

have good news delivered to you by a dove like Noah?

1 KING 17 & GENESIS 8

Would you rather

dream that the sun, moon, and stars bow down to you like Joseph

OR

have his ability to interpret other people's dreams?

GENESIS 37 & GENESIS 40

Would you rather

see a giant bread loaf knocking over your tent

OR

birds eating from bread baskets on your head?

JUDGES 7 & GENESIS 40

Would you rather

see the flaming sword guarding the Tree of Life in Eden

OR

the sun stand still during Joshua's battle?

GENESIS 3 & JOSHUA 10

Would you rather

be guided by God as a pillar of cloud and fire like the Israelites

OR

be led by a star to the newborn Jesus like the Magi?

EXODUS 13 & MATTHEW 2

Would you rather

climb the ladder like the angels in Jacob's dream

OR

be taken up in a whirlwind like Elijah?

GENESIS 28 & 2 KINGS 2

Would you rather

eat a scroll with God's message on it like Ezekiel

OR

eat unleavened bread for seven days during Passover like the Israelites?

EZEKIEL 3 & EXODUS 12

Would you rather

see a donkey talk

OR

an invisible hand write on the wall?

NUMBERS 22 & DANIEL 5

DREAMS AND SYMBOLS

Would you rather

see God's promise as a rainbow in the clouds like Noah

OR

God's provision as a ram in the bush like Abraham?

GENESIS 9 & GENESIS 22

Would you rather

see a sign from God in wet wool on dry ground like Gideon

OR

in fire that soaks up water like Elijah?

JUDGES 6 & 1 KINGS 18

Would you rather

have a dream that your sibling will rule over you like Joseph's brothers

OR

that you will lose your kingdom like King Nebuchadnezzar?

GENESIS 37 & DANIEL 4

Would you rather

have a dream of seven fat cows swallowing seven skinny cows

OR

seven heads of ripe wheat eating seven heads of rotten wheat?

GENESIS 41

Would you rather

be with the disciples to perform miracles

OR

see Moses and Elijah appear with Jesus on the mountain?

MARK 6 & MATTHEW 17

Would you rather

be given a garment of praise

OR

a crown of beauty to take away your sadness?

ISAIAH 61

Would you rather

be warned like Noah of a worldwide flood

OR

warned like Abraham that a big fire will consume your city?

GENESIS 6 & GENESIS 18

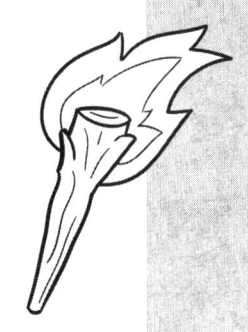

Would you rather

have a dream of four scary beasts like Daniel

OR

of a great famine in the land like Pharaoh?

DANIEL 7 & GENESIS 41

DREAMS AND SYMBOLS

Would you rather

have your staff blossom overnight into an almond tree

OR

turn into a snake like Aaron's?

NUMBERS 17 & EXODUS 7

ROUND 3 WINNER

_____

4

Heroes!

Would you rather

survive a flood of the entire earth at 600 years old like Noah

OR

lead a nation through the Red Sea in your 80s like Moses?

GENESIS 7 & EXODUS 14

Would you rather

care for sheep in the hills like David

OR

gather grain in the fields like Ruth?

1 SAMUEL 16 & RUTH 2

Would you rather

have the supernatural strength of Samson

OR

dance with all your might to praise God like David?

JUDGES 14 & 2 SAMUEL 6

Would you rather

grow up to become royalty like Queen Esther

OR

to be a political leader like Joseph?

ESTHER 2 & GENESIS 41

Would you rather

honor God by only eating vegetables and drinking water like Daniel

OR

only eating locusts and honey like John the Baptist?

DANIEL 1 & MATTHEW 3

Would you rather

have a staff that performs miracles like Aaron's

OR

play a lyre that drives away evil spirits like David's?

VERSES: EXODUS 7 & 1 SAMUEL 16

Would you rather

be trusted to give advice to Moses

OR

be trusted to raise Jesus like Joseph and Mary?

EXODUS 18 & MATTHEW 1

Would you rather

overhear something that saves the king's life like Mordecai

OR

share dream interpretations that come true in three days like Joseph?

ESTHER 2 & GENESIS 40

Would you rather

live on the ark and care for stinky, noisy sheep

OR

slithering, slippery snakes?

GENESIS 6

Would you rather

have your faith tested by losing everything like Job

OR

being thrown in prison like Joseph?

JOB 2 & GENESIS 39

Would you rather

fight with lions and bears like David

OR

wrestle with God like Jacob?

1 SAMUEL 17 & GENESIS 32

Would you rather

have a fancy coat like Joseph

OR

long, flowing hair like Samson that can't be cut?

GENESIS 37 & JUDGES 16

HEROES!

Would you rather

build an ark to save the animals and your family like Noah

OR

defend and rebuild the walls of Jerusalem like Nehemiah?

GENESIS 6 & NEHEMIAH 2

Would you rather

flee your country to hide baby Jesus like Joseph

OR

risk your life to hide spies in your home like Rahab?

MATTHEW 2 & JOSHUA 2

Would you rather

lead the nation of Egypt through a famine like Joseph

OR

lead the Israelites out of Egypt like Moses?

GENESIS 41 & EXODUS 12

Would you rather

walk unharmed in the fiery furnace like Shadrach, Meshach, and Abednego

OR

be lifted unharmed out of the lion's den like Daniel?

DANIEL 3 & DANIEL 6

Would you rather

have the courage to stand before the king like Queen Esther

OR

a giant like young David?

ESTHER 5 & 1 SAMUEL 17

ROUND 4 WINNER

_____

5
Battles

Would you rather

be the solider who kneeled to drink water and could go home

OR

the solider who cupped their hands to drink water and stayed to fight?

JUDGES 7

Would you rather

tell your friends you defeated your enemy with a rock and a slingshot like David

OR

with a donkey's jawbone like Samson?

1 SAMUEL 17 & JUDGES 15

Would you rather

win a battle by pointing your javelin at a city like Joshua

OR

holding your arms up while everyone fights below like Moses?

JOSHUA 8 & EXODUS 17

Would you rather

have your army thrown into panic like Sisera's

OR

Would you rather fall into a tar pit like the men of Sodom and Gomorrah?

JUDGES 4 & GENESIS 14

BATTLES

Would you rather

be the dagger stuck in King Eglon's belly

OR

the stone that sunk into Goliath's forehead?

JUDGES 3 & 1 SAMUEL 17

Would you rather

win a battle by being silent for six days like those at Jericho

OR

by fasting and singing like Jehoshaphat and his kingdom?

JOSHUA 6 & 2 CHRONICLES 20

Would you rather

go to battle with torches hidden in jars

OR

have hornets go ahead of you to attack your enemies?

JUDGES 7 & EXODUS 23

Would you rather

be strong enough to lead only 300 men in battle

OR

be strong enough to pull down the pillars of the temple?

JUDGES 7 & JUDGES 16

Would you rather

have God hurl large hailstones at your foes

OR

send down fire from heaven?

JOSHUA 10 & 2 KINGS 1

Would you rather

your prayers bring an angel of the Lord to fight your enemies

OR

fire from heaven to burn up a wet offering?

2 KINGS 19 & 1 KINGS 18

Would you rather

lead others into battle with the wisdom of Deborah

OR

fight in battles as a trusted and faithful warrior like Uriah the Hittite?

JUDGES 4 & 2 SAMUEL 11

Would you rather

be a skilled archer like the soldiers at the battle of Ramoth-Gilead

OR

great with a slingshot like the left-handed Benjamites?

1 KINGS 22 & JUDGES 20

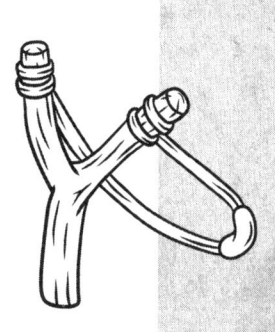

Would you rather

be known for fighting until your hand freezes to your sword like Eleazar

OR

defeating a huge Egyptian with his own spear like Benaiah?

2 SAMUEL 23

Would you rather

conquer and win 60 cities like Moses

OR

be given an earring from every soldier's plunder like Gideon?

DEUTERONOMY 3 & JUDGES 8

Would you rather

rebuild and defend a wall like Nehemiah

OR

pray and march for a wall to come down like Joshua?

NEHEMIAH 2 & JOSHUA 6

Would you rather

lose your thumbs and big toes like Adoni-Bezek

OR

lose the blessing of God like Saul?

JUDGES 1 & 1 SAMUEL 13

Would you rather

be chosen by the Lord to fight against the Midianites like Gideon

OR

chosen to lead the Israelites to the Promised Land like Joshua?

JUDGES 6 & JOSHUA 1

ROUND 5 WINNER

_____

6 Miracles

Would you rather

be spoken to by your donkey like Balaam

OR

warned by an eagle like John?

NUMBERS 22 & REVELATION 8

Would you rather

come home to a bed full of frogs

OR

a field full of locusts like the Egyptians?

EXODUS 8 & EXODUS 10

Would you rather

make poison in a pot disappear like Elisha

OR

casually shake off a snake and survive the bite like Paul?

2 KINGS 4 & ACTS 28

Would you rather

survive being eaten by a big fish

OR

strike a rock and make drinking water come out of it?

JONAH 2 & NUMBERS 20

Would you rather

see God set the sun, moon, and stars in the sky

OR

command the sun and moon to stand still like Joshua?

GENESIS 1 & JOSHUA 10

Would you rather

suddenly fluently speak a different language like the people at the Tower of Babel

OR

not be able to speak until your son is born like Zechariah?

GENESIS 11 & LUKE 1

Would you rather

have Jesus cure your mother's fever

OR

raise your brother from the dead?

MATTHEW 8 & JOHN 11

Would you rather

escape prison with the help of an angel like Peter

OR

escape from Egypt through the Red Sea like the Israelites?

ACTS 12 & EXODUS 14

Would you rather

taste water that revives your strength

OR

taste wine that had once been water?

JUDGES 15 & JOHN 2

Would you rather

be able to make heavy things float like Elisha

OR

water pour out of rocks like Moses?

2 KINGS 6 & EXODUS 17

Would you rather

eat quail until it comes out of your nose like the Israelites

OR

catch so many fish that your boat begins to sink like the fishermen?

NUMBERS 11 & LUKE 5

Would you rather

walk after being bedridden for eight years like Aeneas

OR

cured and given fifteen more years to live like Hezekiah?

ACTS 9 & 2 KINGS 20

Would you rather

have the strength to defeat a lion like Samson

OR

walk for 40 days and 40 nights like Elijah?

JUDGES 14 & 1 KINGS 19

Would you rather

taste the manna that fell from heaven

OR

the bread that was multiplied to feed the 5,000?

EXODUS 16 & JOHN 6

Would you rather

pay your debts with
jars full of olive oil

OR

with money you found
in a fish's mouth?

2 KINGS 4 & MATTHEW 17

Would you rather

be healed by a cleansing in the
Jordan River like Naaman

OR

by having Jesus put spit and mud
on your eyes like the blind man?

2 KINGS 5 & MARK 8

Would you rather

be healed from your sickness by Peter's shadow

OR

by Paul's handkerchief?

ACTS 5 & ACTS 19

ROUND 6 WINNER

_____

7

Jesus' Birth, Life, and Death

Would you rather
be the star that led the Magi to baby Jesus

OR

the angel that appeared to the shepherds and told them about Jesus' birth?

MATTHEW 2 & LUKE 2

Would you rather
race to Jesus' empty tomb like John

OR

swim to the resurrected Jesus on the beach like Peter?

JOHN 20 & JOHN 21

Would you rather

be healed by Jesus' touch like the leper

OR

be healed by his words from a distance like the servant?

MATTHEW 8

Would you rather

not eat for 40 days

OR

sleep outside without a tent for 40 days?

MATTHEW 4

Would you rather

worship baby Jesus in the manger with the Magi

OR

worship Jesus riding into Bethlehem with the crowd?

MATTHEW 2 & MATTHEW 21

Would you rather

see Jesus dunked under water at his baptism

OR

see him walk on water toward the disciples?

LUKE 3 & JOHN 6

Would you rather

get gold at your birth

OR

have thousands of people cheer when you come to town?

MATTHEW 2 & JOHN 12

Would you rather

have people constantly question who you are

OR

have everyone know your name?

MATTHEW 16 & JOHN 12

Would you rather

always start your day by preaching to large crowds

OR

always end your day by driving demons out of people and healing the sick?

MATTHEW 8

Would you rather

be missing for three days as a child

OR

be followed by crowds everywhere you go?

LUKE 2 & MARK 3

Would you rather

be asked to leave a town after helping it

OR

be denied by your friend after loving them?

MATTHEW 8 & LUKE 22

Would you rather

travel for ministry only by walking

OR

by going from boat to boat?

LUKE 8 & MARK 4

Would you rather

be able to pass through
any crowd

OR

be able to pass as someone else?

LUKE 4 & JOHN 20

Would you rather

talk with people already in heaven

OR

be able to talk to your friends
on earth after you die?

MATTHEW 17 & JOHN 20

Would you rather

have a cousin who eats bugs like John the Baptist

OR

a friend who is always falling asleep like Peter?

MATTHEW 3 & MATTHEW 26

Would you rather

teach a lesson by flipping over tables

OR

by talking and writing in the dust?

MATTHEW 21 & JOHN 8

JESUS' BIRTH, LIFE, AND DEATH

Would you rather

have your eyes opened for the first time like the man born blind

OR

your bleeding ear immediately healed like the servant in the garden?

JOHN 9 & LUKE 22

ROUND 7 WINNER

_____

8 Parables

Would you rather

work for nine hours but get paid as if you only worked three hours

OR

not work at all?

MATTHEW 20

Would you rather

be a plant without enough soil

OR

a plant with too much sun?

MARK 4

Would you rather

have everything you've hidden be found

OR

every secret of yours be told?

MATTHEW 10

Would you rather

have a large harvest without enough workers to bring it in

OR

enough workers but a harvest full of weeds?

MATTHEW 9 & MATTHEW 13

Would you rather

have a speck of sawdust in your eye

OR

try to take a speck of sawdust out of someone else's eye?

MATTHEW 7

Would you rather

be the lost sheep found by the Good Shepherd

OR

the beaten traveler found by the Good Samaritan?

LUKE 15 & LUKE 10

Would you rather

have a field with a pearl of great value

OR

hidden treasure?

MATTHEW 13

Would you rather

always have a tear in your clothing that gets worse

OR

drink from bottles that will always break?

MATTHEW 9

Would you rather

be surprised by a last-minute invitation to a fancy wedding banquet

OR

throw a party and surprise strangers by inviting them?

LUKE 14

Would you rather

have a field of rocky soil to plant your crops in

OR

a field of thorns?

MATTHEW 13

Would you rather

be given one large stone

OR

a big snake for your birthday?

MATTHEW 7

Would you rather

have a friend who always says no but eventually does what you ask

OR

a friend who always says yes but never does what you ask?

MATTHEW 21

Would you rather

have to leave the party because you didn't follow the dress code

OR

miss the party because you came too late?

MATTHEW 22 & MATTHEW 25

Would you rather

always get everything you ask for

OR

always find everything you're looking for?

MATTHEW 7

Would you rather

only use salt that
never tastes salty

OR

only be able to plant trees
that grow bad fruit?

MATTHEW 5 & LUKE 6

Would you rather

see a wolf trying to dress
itself as a sheep

OR

a camel trying to fit
through the eye of a
needle?

MATTHEW 7 & MARK 10

PARABLES

Would you rather

spend the day sweeping your house to find a lost coin

OR

making bread from 60 pounds of dough?

LUKE 15 & MATTHEW 13

ROUND 8 WINNER

_____

9

Fruit of the Spirit

Would you rather

give someone your favorite coat who already took your shirt?

OR

let someone slap both your cheeks?

MATTHEW 6

Would you rather

always say hello to people who never say it back

OR

always go for long walks with someone who likes to talk?

MATTHEW 5

Would you rather

stop worrying for an entire month

OR

not judge anyone you know for an entire year?

MATTHEW 7

Would you rather

always know what to say

OR

always know what to do?

MATTHEW 10

Would you rather
be arrested for your faith

OR

chased out of town because of it?

MATTHEW 10

Would you rather
be humble

OR

full of forgiveness?

LUKE 17 & MATTHEW 5

Would you rather

have your righteousness turn you into a good fish

OR

turn you into a good sheep?

MATTHEW 13 & MATTHEW 25

Would you rather

sell everything you own and give the money to the poor

OR

leave your family and home behind to serve others?

MATTHEW 19

FRUIT OF THE SPIRIT

Would you rather

easily forgive your siblings

OR

easily confront your friends?

MATTHEW 5 & MATTHEW 18

Would you rather

spend time praying alone in your room

OR

spend time praying on a mountainside?

MATTHEW 6 & MATTHEW 14

Would you rather

have a show-and-tell where everyone sees the inside of your mouth

OR

the inside of your heart?

LUKE 6

Would you rather

show love to your neighbor by washing their feet like Jesus and the disciples

OR

by giving them your clothes?

JOHN 13 & MATTHEW 25

Would you rather

be disguised as a shrewd snake

OR

as an innocent dove?

MATTHEW 10

Would you rather

have your light shine so brightly that your friends have to wear sunglasses

OR

make so much peace that other people always want to be around you?

MATTHEW 5 & MATTHEW 10

Would you rather

have unending joy for a year

OR

no worries for a year?

NEHEMIAH 8 & PHILIPPIANS 4

Would you rather

have a faith that moves a mountain

OR

a faith that multiplies every seed you plant?

MATTHEW 17 & 2 CORINTHIANS 9

Would you rather

be able to always lend without expecting anything back

OR

always able to love others as well as you love yourself?

LUKE 6 & MARK 12

ROUND 9 WINNER

_____

10 traditions

Would you rather

be baptized in a river like Jesus

OR

inside of your church?

MARK 1

Would you rather

serve at your church with a big group of people

OR

serve behind the scenes?

ACTS 2

Would you rather

share a meal with your friends and family on the Sabbath

OR

spend time alone with God in prayer and Bible reading?

EXODUS 20

Would you rather

not eat meat on Fridays during Lent

OR

give up your favorite snack for 40 days?

MARK 1

Would you rather

put a jumbo nativity scene on your front lawn during Christmas

OR

a supersized Advent wreath?

LUKE 1

Would you rather

attend a worship night with only gospel music

OR

one with only Christian rock?

PSALM 150

Would you rather

wave your palm leaves in the air on Palm Sunday

OR

weave them into a cross?

JOHN 12

Would you rather

teach Sunday school to toddlers

OR

officiate everyone's wedding?

2 TIMOTHY 3 & JOHN 2

TRADITIONS

Would you rather

talk about Jesus with one stranger

OR

share your story of getting to know Jesus with a large audience?

ACTS 14

Would you rather

fellowship by visiting Christians in another country

OR

by visiting Christians at a local church?

ACTS 13

Would you rather

lead an early-morning prayer group

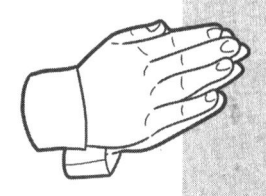

OR

cook and host a dinner for your church family?

ACTS 2

Would you rather

direct your church's annual Christmas play

OR

be a part of the cast?

LUKE 2

Would you rather

eat an entire king's cake to celebrate Epiphany

OR

dress up like one of the Magi?

MATTHEW 2

Would you rather

organize an offering to buy toys for children without gifts

OR

buy food to give to your local pantry to help feed the hungry for Christmas?

ISAIAH 58

Would you rather

only be able to go to a 10:00 a.m. church service

OR

only able to attend a 6:00 p.m. service?

ROMANS 10

Would you rather

be able to know who all of your tithes helped

OR

who all of your prayers changed?

DEUTERONOMY 14 & 1 TIMOTHY 2

Would you rather

worship God by singing as long as you live

OR

by dancing and playing instruments?

PSALM 104 & PSALM 149

ROUND 10 WINNER

_____

tiebreaker

Would you rather
witness Jesus' first miracle, turning water into wine

OR

attend the Last Supper before Jesus' death and resurrection?

JOHN 2 & LUKE 22

TALLY UP
Score Sheets

Name	Score

Name	Score

Name	Score

Name	Score

Winner's Certificate

This certificate is
awarded to

_____

For an exceptional performance of
Would You Rather? Bible Questions!

FINAL SCORE   DATE

Create Your Own!

Would you rather
_____
_____
OR
_____
_____ ?

Would you rather

_____

_____

OR

_____

_____ **?**

Would you rather

_____

_____

OR

_____

_____ **?**

CREATE YOUR OWN!

Would you rather

_____

_____

OR

_____

_____ **?**

Would you rather

_____

_____

OR

_____

_____ **?**

CREATE YOUR OWN!

Would you rather

_____

_____

OR

_____

_____ ?

Would you rather

_____

_____

OR

_____

_____ ?

CREATE YOUR OWN!

Would you rather

_____

_____

OR

_____

_____ **?**

Would you rather

_____

_____

OR

_____

_____ **?**

CREATE YOUR OWN!

Would you rather

_____

_____

OR

_____

_____ ?

Would you rather

_____

_____

OR

_____

_____ ?

CREATE YOUR OWN!

Would you rather

_____

_____

OR

_____

_____ **?**

Would you rather

_____

_____

OR

_____

_____ **?**

CREATE YOUR OWN!

Would you rather

_____

_____

OR

_____

_____ **?**

Would you rather

_____

_____

OR

_____

_____ **?**

CREATE YOUR OWN!

About the Author

Clareese Saunders is a New Jersey–born, Queens-based, second-generation social worker practicing in New York City schools. When she's not being schooled on the latest trends by her students, she's likely relaxing with her amazing quarantine cats, Lily and Mosley. She is passionate about storytelling, community, and growth and connecting it all back to Jesus and his amazing grace. She is incredibly grateful for her vibrant community of family and friends and is always excited to meet and learn from those outside of it.

Hi, parents and caregivers,

We hope your child enjoyed *Would You Rather? Bible Questions*. If you have any questions or concerns about this book, or have received a damaged copy, please contact customerservice@penguinrandomhouse.com. We're here and happy to help. Also, please consider writing a review on your favorite retailer's website to let others know what you and your child thought of the book!

Sincerely,

The Zeitgeist Team

Don't miss these Godly reads—fun for the whole family!

God Is in Nature!
by Jessica Doebler

Connect with God and His awesome creations with 100 devotions for kids! Explore and appreciate all the places God has created, featuring Scripture, Bible studies, creative prompts, and prayers.

"By connecting creation to our wonderful Creator, kids will be drawn to God's incredible love."
—STEVE HILL, LEAD PASTOR, GRACE COMMUNITY FELLOWSHIP

Children's Bible Stories for Bedtime
by Julie Lavender

Wind down with inspiring children's Bible stories and connect with God at bedtime. Immerse young minds in God's Word with full-page illustrations, reflections, and essential stories from the Old and New Testaments.

"The engaging Bible stories are written with kid-friendly, contemporary language while staying true to Scripture."
—CRYSTAL BOWMAN, BESTSELLING AND AWARD-WINNING AUTHOR OF MORE THAN 100 BOOKS FOR CHILDREN

Hardcover gift edition also available now!

zeitgeistpublishing.com